Best UCAS Personal Statement

Law

Copyright

Copyright © 2015 by Chris Christofi
Revised 2016
All rights reserved. This includes the right to reproduce any portion of this booklet in any form.
Self published with CreateSpace by Chris Christofi
First printing in 2016
ISBN-13: 978-1540394859
ISBN-10: 1540394859

LAW

These courses cover core subjects, like tort and criminal law. Other areas of study may include: case law, contract law, land/property law, equity/trusts law, European law, human rights law and public/constitutional law

'Law should govern' - Aristotle

Booklets in this series

Best UCAS Personal Statement: ARCHITECTURE

Best UCAS Personal Statement: BIOLOGICAL SCIENCES/BIOLOGY

Best UCAS Personal Statement: BUSINESS STUDIES

Best UCAS Personal Statement: EDUCATION STUDIES & TEACHER TRAINING

Best UCAS Personal Statement: ENGINEERING/ENGINEERING SCIENCES

Best UCAS Personal Statement: ENGLISH

Best UCAS Personal Statement: GENERAL ADVICE

Best UCAS Personal Statement: LAW

Best UCAS Personal Statement: MEDICINE

Best UCAS Personal Statement: SPORTS SCIENCES/STUDIES

Best UCAS Personal Statement: PSYCHOLOGY

Best UCAS Personal Statement: TEN ORIGINAL PERSONAL STATEMENTS

Forthcoming titles:

Best UCAS Personal Statement: COMPUTER COURSES

Best UCAS Personal Statement: ECONOMICS

Best UCAS Personal Statement: GEOGRAPHY

Best UCAS Personal Statement: HISTORY

Best UCAS Personal Statement: MATHEMATICS

Contents

Acknowledgements 1
Introduction 2
Practical Advice for Students Writing their Personal Statement 6
Getting the Structure Right 14
Useful Skills and Qualities for HE 19
Work Experience/Shadowing/Visits 22
Subject Specific Points to Include 23
Important Experience, Knowledge, Abilities, Skills and Qualities for Law Courses 29
Useful Websites for Law Courses 33
Background Reading for Law Courses 34
Generally Useful Websites for HE Applicants 38
Skills, Qualities and Experiences that Admissions Tutors are Looking for 49
Grid to Collate Information on Skills, Qualities And Experiences 51
Personal Statement Questionnaire 52
Example of Law Personal Statement 63
Bibliography 67
The Author 69

Acknowledgements

Expertise in any area requires not only personal endeavour but the culmination of learning from others and practical experience.

As a Head of Sixth Form for 20 years and an adviser to students on their university applications for some 30 or more years, much of what I have learnt comes from working closely with Year 11 and Sixth Form students. These students have taught me as much as I have taught them.

The detailed expertise and knowledge, though, mainly comes from university staff. The scores of presentations, workshops and lectures by knowledgeable Admissions Tutors I have attended have given me the skills and necessary knowledge to help my own students. Also, a wealth of information is made available by universities through their literature and websites. Here, I hope to put some of this knowledge and experience in writing to help students more broadly.

My best sounding board for what works has been my sons, Antony, Alex and Adam, whose encouragement, criticisms and direction have been invaluable. Last, but not least, I must thank my friend and colleague, Jim Johnson, who worked closely with me for many years on my school's HE and aspirations programme.

Introduction

Every year each round of UCAS applications commences on 1st September. Whether students secure the university place of their choice very much depends on them achieving the required grades. But grades are only part of the story. For many years now, the number of university applications has continued to rise. An exception to the overall trend was a decrease in the number of applications in 2012 (thought to be related to higher fees). But since then, the number of applicants has continued to grow. This means that in many areas, competition is strong. For more competitive courses, the Personal Statement takes on an even more important role.

Admissions Tutors use a variety of information to decide who should be made an offer. They will consider any of the following:

- **GCSE grades** achieved.
- **AS and A2 grades** achieved/predicted or their equivalents (some universities, normally the ones that are more difficult to get into, will look to see if a student has taken resits).
- The **reference**. Students must make sure that they discuss with their referee (the person who writes the reference) things that they have done that their referee may not be aware of. I suggest that students

make a list of their attributes, experiences, achievements and interests. This booklet will show you how information for your Personal Statement can be collected (see the Personal Statement Questionnaire). Most referees would welcome this information since it makes the task of writing a reference much easier.

- Relevant **work experience**. This is particularly relevant for vocational courses. But all students benefit from having relevant work experience/work shadowing.
- The **interview**. This is very important but not all universities interview. This makes the Personal Statement even more important. For many students, the Personal Statement may be their only opportunity to show what type of person they are.
- Some courses (normally, the more demanding ones) require a particular score in an **entry test**.
- The **Personal Statement**. This is the only opportunity most students will have to sell themselves but left to their own devices many students do a poor job.

The Sutton Trust (December 2012) found discrepancies in the quality of Personal Statements submitted by state and public school students. State school students are more likely to make mistakes on their forms and often do not refer to suitable work experience. It is not surprising, therefore, that public school students, with the better Personal Statements, have a better chance of getting into elite universities and onto competitive courses.

What will Admissions Tutors be looking for?

Individual Admissions Tutors have their own personal ideas about recruiting potential applicants, but the list that follows outlines the criteria that most will be using.

- The student's academic potential and strong desire to study the course
- That the student is applying for the right course and will benefit from the course
- Students know the content of the degree course they are applying for and do not express an interest in areas not offered (university websites provide entry profiles for courses)
- A student has the experience, knowledge, abilities and skills that relate to the course (see **Important experience, knowledge, abilities, skills and qualities** for chosen course)
- Motivation and commitment for chosen course (see **Subject Specific Points to Include** for chosen course)

- Creativity
- Ability to work independently
- An individual's industry and commitment to successfully complete the course
- How an applicant will fit in as an individual
- An individual's potential positive contribution to the university and university life
- An individual's potential to contribute positively to the course

Students who do not convince Admission Tutors on the first of the five points above represent common reasons for rejection.
If you really impress the Admissions Tutor, you are more likely to secure the place of your dreams. You may even (although it does not happen often) get lowered grade offers!

The application process is a competitive one and like any competition, you need to ensure that all elements are undertaken and completed as well as they can be. Overall, in Law courses, for approximately every 5.2 applicants, only 1 is accepted.

Practical Advice for Students Writing their Personal Statement

Remember:

- A Personal Statement must not be more than 4,000 characters (including spaces) or 47 lines of text (this includes blank lines).
- Aim for around 70%-80% of the Personal Statement to be about the course that is chosen (include information on knowledge, qualities, skills, interests and experiences that relate to the course). This figure is only there to suggest that the bulk of the Personal Statement should be about how you are suitable to study Law courses.
- Provide evidence to support personal qualities, knowledge, experiences and skills. Use university websites to establish exactly what the Admissions Tutors are looking for. Address what they are looking for in your Personal Statement.
- Only refer to A Levels (or equivalent courses) to highlight how they support your interest in the course you are applying for or why you chose a particular combination.
- Base your writing on your intended course(s).

- Ensure what you say is always relevant.
- Provide evidence for your claims. For example, do not just say: *'I am a good communicator.'* It is better to write: *'I have, for two years running, won first prize in Youth Speaks competitions.'*
- Keep the structure and language simple.
- Do not use words you do not understand.
- Keep your sentences short (particularly if writing is not your strength).
- Punctuate carefully.
- Check your spelling and grammar.
- Exclamation marks (!) should rarely be used, if at all.
- Be positive. Always talk about what you have done and achieved, not what you intend to do (unless it is planned) or have not had the opportunity to achieve.
- Be honest and enthusiastic.
- Make your application read like an interesting professional application.
- Do not boast – the referee can do this for you. It counts a lot more if it is done this way.
- Do not appear arrogant. There is a fine line between coming across as confident and appearing arrogant or overconfident. Another person reading your draft is more likely to pick this up.
- Tailor your Personal Statement to your

specific courses. If it is a combined course, you will have to use criteria for both subjects.
- Ensure what you write is always relevant. You do not have the space to go off at a tangent.
- Show you are mature and have your own ideas.
- Come across as a well-rounded individual.
- Proof read (or ask somebody else to do it) carefully. And then, proof read again. Keep doing this until you get it right.
- When you read back your Personal Statement, the person that comes through must be the real you.
- If they interview for your course, it is very likely that some of the interview questions will be based on your Personal Statement. This needs to be at the back of your mind when compiling your Personal Statement.
- Only include things that will improve your chances of getting onto your chosen course.

Avoid:

- Using headings (they take up too many valuable words).
- Waffle.
- Lying.

- Generalising (be specific and support your points with examples).
- Trying to sound clever, eg by giving long meaningless quotes that you may not even understand; by making unsupported claims, or by using unfamiliar language.
- Listing courses and exam results.
- Producing long lists of things you have read or done. The important things are what you have learnt or what skills you demonstrated when you have undertaken various things, or what opinions you have formed.
- Making unqualified statements, like 'I enjoy reading.'
- Repetition. This applies to repeating words and ideas. Use a thesaurus if necessary.
- Avoid being boring (the best way to do this is by following the advice in this booklet).
- Making unhelpful statements like: 'I enjoy watching the TV,' 'I go to clubs with my friends,' 'I enjoy the pub.'
- Copying from other people's Personal Statement (UCAS has a means of checking).
- Clichés.
- Avoid starting too many sentences with 'I.' So, instead of: *'I have captained the first eleven football team ......'* write: *'Having captained the first eleven football team ....'*
- Quotes should only ever be used if they add something genuine to the

Personal Statement. Normally, they do not. A Personal Statement should be about you.
- Being modest and underselling yourself.
- Using colloquialisms (slang).
- Avoid trying to sound funny.
- Do not give irrelevant personal anecdotes.
- Avoid suggesting you are going to do things before university that you have not firmly planned.
- Referring to a specific university or specific university course (other universities will not like it). The only time you can do this is if, for some reason, you have only applied for one course.
- Do not take a particular political standpoint.
- Not making the most of the characters available and making the Personal Statement too short.

It is not unusual for students with three A grades at A2 not to get into their first choice course. Many students find writing a difficult chore and need help. This booklet provides the means of supporting both the tutor/higher education adviser and the student to produce a Personal Statement that is both fit for purpose and also one that maximises a student's chance of achieving their desired university place. At all times, students must be discouraged from plagiarising other people's work. This is not only unethical but is unlikely to lead to a Personal Statement that best 'sells' and reflects a student's potential for a given course.

Personal Statement structure

It is a good idea to collate information first before attempting to write your Personal Statement. Using the **Personal Statement Questionnaire** is one possible way of organising information before writing the Personal Statement.

Make sure you have a predetermined structure to your Personal Statement. A possible layout could be:

1. **Introduction.** Why do I want to do this course? Show an understanding of what the course involves (see Subject Specific Points to Include).

2. **Supporting information** which demonstrates a desire to do the course, e.g. background reading (see Subject Specific Points to Include). Refer to skills, experiences and attributes that you have demonstrated and are relevant for the course.

3. **Interests, hobbies, activities and**

responsibilities. What attributes do you have that would be useful for your intended course? (see Subject Specific Points to Include and Useful Skills and Qualities). This can help to show that you are a rounded individual.

4. **Concluding.** A strong statement is needed about the reasons for applying for the course. This can be linked to future career intentions or ambitions.

Use the subject and general criteria to draft your first copy. It is a good idea to save the Personal Statement as a word document and then transfer the final draft onto the electronic form. Do not forget to back-up your work.

You can use the above structure to help you shape your work into a logical and coherent order. It is not the only way to structure a Personal Statement, but unless you are particularly good at writing and structuring work, you may find it is a good idea to adhere to this structure.

Complete the questionnaire and use the information to produce your first draft. The first draft is rarely the finished product. Go through your first draft and check for spelling, punctuation and grammar. Also check that you are not repeating the same words too often. Use a dictionary and thesaurus to help you. If too many sentences begin with 'I,' see if you can find alternative ways to write some of the sentences.

Ensure that you have the desired structure and that your work 'flows.' Now you are ready for the third draft! At this stage, it is useful to get someone, like a tutor, parent, etc to check your work. Further drafts may be needed. This booklet you are reading has been through approximately 30 drafts! It is advisable therefore to start this process early. I believe it is a good idea to have a first draft ready by the end of July with a view to applying by the end of October of the same year (except for courses where the deadline is 15th October).

Remember, this may be your only opportunity to sell yourself to the Admissions Tutor.

Getting the Structure Right

It will help you if you split your Personal Statement into definite sections.

When writing the different parts of the structure also refer to Subject Specific Points to Include and Important Experience, Knowledge, Abilities, Skills and Qualities for Education Studies & Teacher Training Courses.

1. **Introduction.** This is your opportunity to capture the attention of the reader and make yourself memorable. Why do I want to do this course? This is a very important section. It shows your motivation, commitment and knowledge. A good start often sets the tone for the rest of the Personal Statement. Show an understanding of what the course involves.

   - Give reason(s) for choosing your course
   - What is the background to your interest in this subject?

- You can refer to inspirational reading that has inspired you to want to pursue your chosen course further
- Give specific areas of interest in the course you are applying for

2. **Supporting information which demonstrates a desire to do the course, e.g. background reading (see Subject Specific Points to Include). Refer to skills, experiences and attributes that you have demonstrated and are relevant for the course.**
   - List relevant courses, trips, workshops, visits, employment, work experience or shadowing that relate to the course you are applying for. State what you learnt from your experiences and what skills you demonstrated
   - Relevant work experience/shadowing
   - Refer to involvement in: Young Enterprise, Duke of Edinburgh scheme, etc
   - ICT competence
   - Give examples of experiences that demonstrate an interest in your

subject:
- (i) Books, journals, newspapers, magazines (give details of what you have read and make at least some comment on some aspect of it). Refer to the Background Reading for Law courses page for ideas on what to read
- (ii) Interesting and relevant talks
- (iii) A relevant project or piece of coursework you have enjoyed
- (iv) Watching relevant films or documentaries

3. **Interests, hobbies, activities and responsibilities. What attributes do you have that would be useful for your intended course? These activities can help to show that you are a rounded individual. They may also highlight skills that are important for your course.**
   - Comment on sporting, musical, dramatic and artistic achievements and the skills that you developed from the activities, such as team work, leadership, etc
   Membership to a debating society and skills that you developed from it

- Other interests, hobbies or activities that you can use to demonstrate skills that are relevant to studying at HE and your course
- Mention any areas of responsibility and skills you developed in undertaking your role

4. Concluding. **This is your opportunity to make a memorable impression. A strong statement about the reasons for applying for the course is needed. This can be linked to future career intentions or ambitions.**

Some of the suggestions that follow here could also be included earlier on in your Personal Statement.

- State your career aspirations if they relate to the course
- Make a strong statement about what you will gain from your Higher Education studies and what it means to you to do this course
- Comment on how you look forward to the way of working at HE level and skills and attributes you want to develop
- Show that you will flourish socially and academically at university

- Gap year intentions, if relevant (if you are doing something which relates to the course, then highlight it)

There are a number of other structures that may be suggested to you by your tutor, higher education adviser or year head. These are all perfectly acceptable. What all structures will have in common is the Introduction and Conclusion.

Useful Skills and Qualities for HE

<u>Some</u> of these skills and qualities must appear in your Personal Statement. Choose the most relevant qualities for your intended course (see Subject Specific Points to Include). Scrutinise carefully course details in the prospectuses. Your school/college reference should also feature some of these. Say what you have done to demonstrate these skills.

adaptable		energetic
	pragmatic	
ambitious		enterprising
	prioritising	
analytical		helpful
	productive	
approachable		ICT numerate
	punctual	
assertive		imaginative
	realistic	
		independent
attention to detail		
broad minded		industrious
	research	

caring		initiative
	resourceful	
committed		leadership
	responsible	
confident		listening
	self-disciplined	
co-operative		mature
	self-reliant	
conscientious		meeting deadlines
	self-starter	
creative		motivated
	sensitive	
decisive		numerate
	sociable	
dedicated		observant
	stamina	
dependable		oral communication
	tactful	
determined		organised
	talented	
diplomatic		patient
	team player	
disciplined		perseverance
	time management	
efficient		perceptive

trustworthy

emotionally literate   positive
          willingness to learn

empathetic   practical
     written communication

                              reliable

Work Experience/Shadowing/Visits

Early thought, preparation and planning will allow you to get more worthwhile experiences and more breadth in your experiences. 'Early' means beginning to consider things by Year 10. Use 'My personal statement timeline' (on the UCAS website) for a possible plan. It is useful if the experience is directly related to what you want to do but other experiences also give you opportunities to develop and demonstrate useful skills, like industry, initiative, punctuality, reliability, etc.

It is helpful if you can be recommended for a placement, so make use of the people you know to help you find worthwhile experiences. These may include your parents, neighbours, teachers, careers advisers, friends,' parents, GP, etc. Consider carefully how you approach employers: write letters that show professionalism and an eagerness for the role. Rehearse telephone conversations and think carefully about the image you are trying to portray.

Subject Specific Points to Include

Not every individual has had the same experiences and therefore you will have to select the most appropriate points to include in your Personal Statement. The important thing is to demonstrate you have the ability, motivation, interest and appropriate skills and qualities to undertake a course in Law.

Use your Personal Statement to give Admissions Tutors an insight into your potential, interest and creative ability in this subject.

- Explain fully (convincingly) why you want to study Law. Is this something that has arisen from your studies or has some other experience inspired you to want to pursue law?

- Your personal statement should demonstrate an understanding of what your chosen field of study entails and how you can demonstrate you have the qualities (use examples) to study this subject. These are some important skills: initiative, common sense, a practical approach to problem solving, analysis, logical thought, precise working, stamina, critical observation, flexibility, creativity, selecting relevant information, etc. Also, you need to show that you are good with people and have good interpersonal skills

- If you have studied law already, what topics interested you and why? For example, tort law, criminal law, European law, etc

- Try and demonstrate that you are confident, decisive, self motivated with the ability to prioritise your own workload. Show a commitment and readiness to take on responsibility. Comment on any responsibilities you may have, eg Head Boy/Girl, House Captain, etc

- Refer to any experiences which

demonstrate integrity, discretion and confidentiality. If you are a mentor, you may have demonstrated these skills in this role

- Show that you can assimilate facts quickly, work well under pressure and think on your feet

- You need to demonstrate good verbal and written communication skills. If you do classroom assisting, refer to how you explain information to other students. Or, if you have presented information to a group, refer to this. If you are a member of a debating society, comment on the skills you have demonstrated in this role. For example, being persuasive, attention to detail, cogent argument, good listening skills, clear and effective expression and making considered responses

- Demonstrate an interest law: what legal pages of quality newspapers do you read? Refer to one or two articles from quality papers like The

Times (on Tuesdays) and The Independent (on Wednesdays). Also recommended are The Guardian's law pages. Show an awareness of legal issues, particularly any current high profile trials

- Mention examples of books or articles (eg, from Counsel Magazine, The Economist, The Law Society Gazette, etc) you have read (do not just give a long list). Make some relevant comment on the material you have read [refer to the Further reading section for examples of background reading]. Remember, Law involves a large quantity of reading

- Refer with examples to your organisational skills, teamwork and leadership skills. This could be done by highlighting areas of responsibility, such as Head Boy/Girl, prefect, etc or through your role in a team or club

- Mention any work experience or shadowing that is relevant, eg firm of solicitors, barrister's chambers, Citizen's Advice Bureau or law department of a company (describe the type of company). What skills were you using (communication, teamwork, problem solving, IT)?

- Refer to any visits to magistrates' court or Crown Court. What did you observe and learn from these visits?

- Refer to any taster courses you have attended, online university courses, or relevant lectures

- If you have spoken to any solicitors, lawyers, etc, refer to this and say what you learnt

- If your field of study has a foreign language component, refer to your foreign language skills and the potential advantage of possessing such skills in Law

- Teamwork, good leadership and good interpersonal skills (including good communication skills) are very important. How have you demonstrated these?

- If you have done an EPQ in a relevant area, refer to it and state what you have learnt from doing it. This can show commitment and initiative, as well as skills to research independently
- Refer to your career ambitions if they involve you Law degree, eg solicitor, barrister, etc

Important Experience, Knowledge, Abilities, Skills and Qualities for Education Studies & Teacher Training Courses

- knowledge, enthusiasm, commitment and understanding of the course

- Initiative

- Common sense

- A practical approach to problem solving

- Good analytical skills

- Logical

- Precise working

- Stamina
- Critically observant
- Flexible
- Creative
- Good interpersonal skills
- Confident
- Decisive
- Motivated
- Ability to prioritise
- Responsible
- Have integrity
- Show discretion
- Maintain confidentiality
- Assimilate facts quickly

- Work well under pressure
- Think on your feet
- Good verbal and written communication skills
- Persuasive
- Show attention to detail
- Present cogent argument
- Good listening skills
- Clear and effective expression
- Make considered responses
- Background reading
- Good organisational skills
- Teamwork
- Leadership skills

- Ability to research
- Independent learner

Useful websites:

Chambers Student:
http://www.chambersstudent.co.uk/

Crown Prosecution Service (CPS):
www.cps.gov.uk

EPOC Careers Conference: www.epoc.org.uk

Faculty of Advocates: www.advocates.org.uk

General Council of the Bar of England and Wales:
www.barcouncil.org.uk

Institute of Legal Executives: www.ilex.org.uk

Institute of Professional Legal Studies:
www.qub.ac.uk/ipls

Law Careers Advice Network:
http://www.lcan.org.uk/

Law Careers.Net: www.lawcareers.net

Lawyer 2B: www.lawyer2B.com

Law Society of England and Wales:
www.lawsociety.org.uk

Law Society of Northern Ireland: www.lawsoc-ni.org

Law Society of Scotland: www.lawscot.org.uk

National Admissions Test for Law (LNAT): www.lnat.ac.uk

Roll on Friday: www.rollonfriday.com

The Legal Education Foundation: http://www.thelegaleducationfoundation.org/

The Prelaw Course: www.prelaw.org.uk

Further reading

Any background reading that relates to this subject is relevant. Be selective in your reading (read things that inspire you). Choose specific articles or chapters (even parts of chapters) to read.

- A Casebook on Contract – A Burrows, Hart Publishing, 2007
- An Introduction to Law – Phil Harris, Cambridge University Press, 2006
- BBC Website Law in Action www.bbc.co.uk/podcasts/series/law
- British Government and the Constitution – Colin Turpin and Adam Tomkins, Cambridge University Press, 2007
- Careers in Law – Martin Edwards, Kogan Page, 1995
- Criminal Law: Text, Cases and Materials – Jonathan Herring, Oxford University Press, 2012
- Critical Thinking Skills: Developing Effective Analysis and Argument – Stella Cottrell, Palgrave Macmillan, 2011
- Contract Law – E McKendrick, Palgrave Macmillan, 2007 – Catherine Elliott and Frances Quinn, Longman, 2007
- English Legal System – Catherine Elliott

and Frances Quinn, Pearson, 2013
- First Book of English Law – O Hood Phillips, Sweet and Maxwell, 1988
- Future Learn https://www.futurelearn.com/courses/categories/law
- Getting into Law – Lianne Carter, Trotman, 2016
- Hobsons Guide to Careers in Law – Hobsons, 2003
- Information for Lawers www.infolaw.co.uk
- Law and Modern Society – P S Atiyah, Oxford, 1995
- Law Review – three annual issues
- https://www.hoddereducation.co.uk/magazines
- Learning the Law – Glanville Williams and A T H Smith, Sweet and Maxwell, 2010
- Legal Action www.lag.org.uk
- Legal Business www.legalease.co.uk
- Legal Skills – E Finch and S Fafinski, Oxford University Press, 2011
- Letters to a Law Student: a Guide to Studying Law at University – N J McBride, Oxford University Press, 2007
- Studying Law at University: Everything

You Need to Know – Allen & Unwin, 2005
- The Independent (on Wednesday)
- The Art of the Advocate – Richard Du Cann, Penguin, 1980
- The Lawyer http://www.thelawyer.com/
- The Law Machine – Marcel Berlins and Clark Dyer, Penguin, 2000
- The Law Society Gazette www.lawgazette.co.uk
- The Economist www.economist.com/products/subscribe
- The Legal Professional – Elbert Hubbard, Kessinger Publishing, 2010
- The Times (on Tuesday)
- The UCAS Guide to Getting into Law: Information on Careers, Entry Routes and Applying to University and College, UCAS, 2012
- Tort Law – Kirsty Horsey and Erica Rackley, Oxford University Press, 2013
- Understanding Company Law – A Hudson, Routledge, 2012
- Understanding the Law – Geoffrey Rivlin, Oxford University Press, 2012
- Working in Law – Charlie Phillips, Trotman, 2011

Generally Useful Websites for HE Applicants

General Advice

All About College (www.allaboutcollege.com)

Government Website (www.direct.gov.uk/en/EducationAndLearning)

Guardian Education (www.education.guardian.co.uk)

Guide to life and learning (www.hcstuff.com)

HE and Research opportunities in UK (www.hero.co.uk)

HE information (www.aimhigher.com)

Higher Education Statistics Agency (www.hesa.ac.uk)

Interactive careers education guidance (www.fasttomato.com.uk)

Intute (helps you find the best websites for study and research) (www.intute.ac.uk)

National Union of Students (www.nus.org.uk)

Push Online (www.push.co.uk)

Student Book (courses, universities and fees) (www.studentguidebook.co.uk)

Times Online (www.timesonline.co.uk)

Unistats (for comparing courses) (http://unistats.direct.gov.uk)

University courses

Admissions service for the Republic of Ireland (www.cao.ie)

Choosing a university (and more) (www.university.which.co.uk)

Course search data base (www.hotcourses.com)

Courses/tariff points/open days (www.coursediscover.co.uk)

Foundation degrees (www.fd.ucas.com)

Full range of services on offer on UCAS Connect (www.ucasconnect.com)

Guardian education (http://education.guardian.co.uk)

UCAS course search (www.ucas.com)

UK Course Finder (www.ukcoursefinder.com)

Course suitability

Kudos (www.cascaid.co.uk)

The Morrisby Profile (www.morrisby.com)

Finding an HE focus

Centigrade Online (www.centigradeonline.co.uk)

Icould is about inspiration for your career (www.icould.com)

National learners' database in Ireland (www.qualifax.ie)

Woody's Webwatch (www.woodyswebwatch.com)

Students with disabilities

Facilities and access (www.skill.org.uk)

Open days

University/college open days (www.opendays.com)

University ratings

Guardian University Guide (www.education.guardian.co.uk)

Graduate opportunities

Careers guidance (www.prospects.ac.uk)

Links to careers websites (www.careers-portal.co.uk)

Student and graduate job site (www.thebigchoice.com)

The Times top 100 graduate employers (www.top100graduateemployers.com)

Finance

Brightside Uniaid student calculator (www.studentcalculator.org.uk)

Bursaries/sponsorship (www.hotcourses.com)

Finance overview (www.dfes.gov.uk/studentsupport)

Finance tour (www.gov.uk/unimoney)

Helpful tools and guidance (www.thestudentroom.co.uk/studentfinance)

Information and advice on finance (www.studentfinancedirect.co.uk)

Information for England, Scotland, Northern Ireland (www.direct.gov.uk)

Local authority information (www.dfes.gov.uk/localauthorities)

Non-EU international students (www.ukcisa.org.uk)

Northern Ireland (www.studentfinanceni.co.uk)

Other EU countries
(www.direct.gov.uk/studentfinance)

Planning and organising finances
(www.studentmoney.org)

Scotland
(www.scotland.gov.uk/Topics/Education/UniversitiesColleges/16640/financial-help)

Student loans (www.slc.co.uk)

Wales (www.studentfinancewales.co.uk)

Gap year

Aventure travel for 2 weeks to 2 years
(www.realgap.co.uk)

Expeditions for 6 to 15 weeks
(www.yearoutgroup.org)

Gap year ideas and travel deals
(www.gapyear.com)

Gap year jobs (www.gapyearjobs.co.uk)

Gap year opportunities (www.gap.org.uk)

Group trips for 18 – 35 year-olds (www.contiki.com)

USA opportunities (www.fulbright.co.uk)

Year in Industry (www.yini.org.uk)

Studying abroad

Belgium (some degree courses in Biology, such as business and economics) (www.studyinbelgium.be)

Denmark (lots of business/economics, IT and engineering courses in English) (www.studyindenmark.dk)

Erasmus (exchange programmes in Europe) (www.britishcouncil.org/erasmus.htm)

ESL Language Travel (www.esl.co.uk)

Germany (North American Studies taught in English and many master's programmes) (www.studying-in-germany.org)

Netherlands (courses in English, financial advice and application process) (www.studyholland.co.uk)

Prospects (profiles from students who have studied abroad) (www.prospects.ac.uk)

Sweden (a number of degree courses are taught in English but fees and living costs are expensive) (www.studyinsweden.se)

The Association of Commonwealth Universities (www.acu.ac.uk)

The National Union of Students (www.nus.org.uk)

The Study Options (for studying in Australia and New Zealand) (www.studyoptions.com)

The Complete University Guide (www.thecompleteuniversityguide.co.uk/international/studying-overseas/)

The Top University Website (for study abroad) (www.topuniversities.com)

The UK Council for International Student Affairs (advice for home students studying abroad) (www.ukcisa.org.uk)

UK student programmes abroad (www.study-abroad-uk.com/)

Volunteering

British Trust for Conservation Volunteers:
www.btcv.org.uk

For 16 and 17 year olds
(www.gov.uk/government/get-involved/take-part/national-citizen-service)

Independent charity and membership organisation
(www.volunteering.org.uk)

National Centre for Volunteering:
www.volunteering.org.uk

National Council for Voluntary Organisations:
www.ncvo-vol.org.uk

Northern Ireland volunteering opportunities
(www.volunteernow.co.uk)

Scottish national volunteering centre
(www.volunteerscotland.net)

The UK volunteering and learning charity:
http://volunteerchampions.csv.org.uk/

Volunteering projects across 12 countries
(www.gvi.co.uk)

Volunteering, adventure and work placements overseas (www.gapforce.org)

Volunteering for people and causes that matter to you (www.do-it.org.uk/)

Volunteering Holidays (www.originalvolunteers.co.uk)

Volunteers: https://www.gov.uk/government/get-involved/take-part/volunteer

Voluntary Service Overseas for 18-25 year olds (www.vso.org.uk)

Welsh volunteering opportunities (www.volunteering-wales.net)

Working and volunteering holidays (www.bunac.org)

Distance learning

The Complete University Guide (http://www.thecompleteuniversityguide.co.uk/distance-learning/what-is-distance-learning/)

The Open University (http://www.open.ac.uk/)

Ucas (http://www.ucas.com/how-it-all-works/flexible-study)

Skills, Qualities and Experiences that Admissions Tutors are looking for

You can use the questionnaire that follows to help you to gather information for your Personal Statement. You can then selectively choose the relevant information to include in your final Personal Statement. This information will also be useful for your referee. The UCAS website has an alternative and simpler form that you can use, called the Personal Statement Worksheet.

Before you start completing the questionnaire, go through the course descriptions from the prospectus or UCAS website and list the skills, qualities and experiences that Admissions Tutors are looking for. Open Days are another excellent way to find out what the course requirements are. This is also a very good opportunity to ask questions. The UCAS website will provide you with all the dates

when the Open Days are on.

Your teachers and tutor may be able to identify some of your strengths for you. School reports will often refer to skills and qualities and how they may have been demonstrated.

Grid to collate Information on Skills, Qualities and Experiences

course/HE institution	skills	qualities	experiences	how demonstrated? (using evidence)

Personal Statement Questionnaire

a. Why do you want to do the proposed course?

b. When did you first realise you wanted to study this course and what triggered this interest?

c. What do you enjoy about this subject? Show you understand what the course requires and what makes you a suitable applicant.

Comment on areas of the course you particularly enjoy.

Highlight areas of particular interest – say what interests you and why.

d. What strengths do you have that will make you suitable for this course?

e. Employment record (including paid jobs).

Include any attributes and skills you may have developed from such experience.

List work experience/work shadowing/work related learning/voluntary work. Say how long each experience lasted and when it was undertaken. What abilities, attributes and skills did you demonstrate (link these to the course)?

f. If possible, say how each of the subjects you are studying at advanced level offers knowledge or skills that will help you in your intended university course.

g. Mention any exceptional performances in your studies. For example, it could be Maths challenge, Young Enterprise, success in competitions, etc.

h. Are you planning to defer (give full details of what you plan to do in your year off)? If your experiences will help you in your intended course of study, say what the experiences are and how they will help you.

i. Describe yourself as a student/person. Use some of the key words below to indicate the kind of student you are. Give examples that demonstrate this.

Eg.

In my studies, I am reliable and always aim to meet all my deadlines.

As the Captain of the first eleven football team I play an important role in leading others. I often use praise as well as guidance.

KEY WORDS:

approachable - attention to detail - analytical - caring - cheerful - committed – confident - conscientious - co-operative - creative - decisive - determined - diplomatic – efficient – empathetic - enterprising - enthusiastic - good attendance record - good written/oral communication skills - gregarious - hardworking - helpful - imaginative - independent - initiative -

interpersonal skills - industrious - ICT numerate - leadership - listening – meet deadlines - maturity - motivated - numerate – observant - organised – patient - persevere - prioritising - problem solving - punctual - reliable - research skills - responsible – self-disciplined – sensitive – show initiative - sociable - stamina – team player – time management – trustworthy - willingness to learn - work well as part of a team

j. Give any details of experiences you have had that link to this course. Say what you learnt from these and how they demonstrate your abilities, attributes, personality and skills.

k. Reading: include books (give authors), journals, specific newspaper columns or other reading. Point out things you found interesting in your reading that relate to your proposed course. What makes them interesting? Say if your reading is just for pleasure.

l. Travel: (if any of your experiences relate to your proposed course then point them out here). This is very important for students including foreign languages in their study. Mention any exchange visits. Relate any benefits to your intended course.

m. Voluntary Work:

Examples include vinspired Awards, Worldwide Volunteering Certificate, Project Trust, etc. What did you do and what skills were involved?

n. Lectures: refer to any relevant out of school/college lectures attended. This also includes online courses.

o. Documentaries:

If you watch relevant/inspirational material, give examples of what you have seen and how it links to your intended course of study.

p. Other experiences: (eg, ASDAN, Duke of Edinburgh Award, National Citizen Service, Young Enterprise, Cadet Force, visits, etc).

q. School/college experiences:

If you have undertaken any of the following, give full details, including dates. State the skills you had to use or to develop in order to undertake these roles.

Classroom assisting:

Mentoring:

Sports:

Mention your role or any special awards/achievements. Say if you have participated at County, regional or national level in a sport. Highlight any leadership or teamwork involved.

Music:

Mention your role or any special awards/achievements/grades. Say if you have been involved in any performances.

Drama:

Mention your role or any special awards/achievements. Say if you have been involved in any performances.

Positions of responsibility, eg, prefect, house captain, head boy/girl, etc. State their precise nature and your role – indicate when you had these roles. What skills and attributes were necessary for each role?

Membership to clubs and societies: (If not mentioned earlier, eg, debating society)

Other:

r. Hobbies/Other interests

If you have any other hobbies and interests not already mentioned, list them here. Say what appeals to you about these hobbies/interests. Mention any achievements, eg, Grade 4 guitar, Bronze swimming certificate, etc). What skills were required for these activities?

s. Relaxation

Say how you relax and how you deal with the stress of studying.

t. Fast tracking

If you have been fast tracked and therefore completed your courses earlier, then give details here.

u. Time off studies

If you have taken time off and then gone back to your studies, give details of what you did during your time off.

v. What career do you want to do after you complete your degree or HND? Or, what aspirations do you have? It is useful to link what you are going to gain from the course to future ambitions.

What attracts you to this career?

Example of Law Personal Statement

You must not copy any part of this page. Your own Personal Statement must be original. The word 'personal' suggests that your Personal Statement must reflect you (your plans, ambitions, attributes, skills and knowledge).

My fascination with Law comes from the belief that the laws of a nation provide the structure and the 'glue' that maintains a functioning society. From ancient times, law makers and philosophers like Aristotle saw the importance of a robust legal system.

My father is French and I was raised to be bilingual. This has given me another dimension to my outlook and an interest in European laws. Through family contacts, I have been able to secure a three month placement in a French law firm, prior to attending university. I also undertook two weeks work experience with a local solicitor. Even though the bulk of the work I did was clerical, the solicitors took the time to give me an insight into the work being undertaken, including company, criminal and property law. Last year I visited the local Magistrates' Court where some crimes for non-payment of debt were tried. Although the Magistrates issued fines, they were sensitive to individuals' circumstances.

I chose my three A levels based on the subjects I enjoyed the most; I believe the skills I am developing will be useful in studying Law. For example, English has improved my communication skills and my ability to debate in a clear and persuasive way. Participating in Youth Speaks has focused me on being an active listener, as well as presenting a cogent argument. In History, I have learnt the importance of objectivity, critical observation and selecting relevant information. My enjoyment of Maths stems from the love of working logically through problems, precise working, analysing and problem solving.

I very much enjoy reading the law pages of The Guardian and The Times. It was very interested to read about the trial of Oscar Pistorius in South Africa between March to October 2014. He killed his girlfriend, Reeva Steenkamp and was eventually found guilty of culpable homicide and sentenced for five years in prison. This was a very public trial with the whole world looking on. At the time, it felt that the trial was been conducted through the media and in public, as much as it was in court. Questions were raised about the role of the media in high profile court cases and whether this interfered with the process of having a fair trial.

My Head of Sixth Form nominated me for my role as a Year 9 mentor and I received training from the local education authority. The role demands good interpersonal skills, as well as integrity and discretion. It is rewarding to have an impact on another student's school work or behaviour. I am also a prefect, where I have to oversee Year 9 students during their school breaks. Good leadership is an important part of this role, but equally important is emotional intelligence and being able to respond to situations with sensitivity.

I regularly play netball for the school and occasionally play football for my village ladies' team. These are my favourite pastimes and I enjoy both the physical activity and the teamwork that is involved in team sports. For the last two years, I have worked on the customer service desk of a local store. This role was given to me because of my ability to deal effectively and courteously with a variety of people.

After attending Law Summer School, my decision to study Law became definite. The Summer School gave me an excellent insight into the study of Law at university. More long term, I am considering becoming a barrister. The idea of advocacy and representing individuals or organisations in court greatly appeals to me. Having said that I would also like to explore and consider other legal careers.

Bibliography

Creating Your UCAS Personal Statement – Alan Bullock, Trotman, 2011

Degree Course and University – Brian Heap, Trotman, 2015

Degree Course Descriptions – John Maidstone and Ken Reynolds (Eds), COA, 2016

40 Successful Personal Statements for UCAS Application – Guy Nobes and Gavin Nobes, Cambridge Occupational Analysts, 2006

How to Write a Winning UCAS Personal Statement – Ian Stannard, The Daily Telegraph & Trotman, 2010

Oxford and Cambridge – Sarah Alakija, Mander Portman Woodward, 2005

Personal Statements – Paul Telfer, Iris Books, 2005

The Big Guide – UCAS, 2014

The Higher-Education Adviser's Handbook – Andy Gardner, Park Parade Publishing, 2006

The Times Good University Guide – John O'Leary, Times Books, 2016

University Degree Course Offers – Brian Heap, Mander Portman Woodward, 2016

University Interviews Guide – Andy Gardner and Barbara Hamnett, Jfs, 2004

The Virgin Alternative Guide to British Universities – Piers Dudgeon, Virgin Publishing Ltd, 2012

Writing a UCAS Personal Statement in Seven Easy Steps – Julia Dolowicz, howtobooks, 2011

Writing an Effective UCAS Personal Statement – Michael Senior and Paul Mannix, Senior Press, 2001

You Want to Study What: Volume I? – Dianah Ellis, Trotman, 2003 [good for those unusual or minority subjects]

You Want to Study What: Volume II? – Dianah Ellis, Trotman, 2003 [good for those unusual or minority subjects]

The Author

Chris Christofi has been a published author since 1988. He is the author and co-author of a number of educational books. He has had a range of educational articles published in newspapers and educational journals.

As a career teacher, Chris progressed from Head of Biology to Head of Sixth Form (for twenty years) to Senior Assistant Headteacher in a large, successful comprehensive school. Having taught for 35 years, Chris stepped down from full-time teaching in 2012, in order to pursue his writing interests. For over 30 years, he has had a responsibility for guiding numerous successful candidates through the university application process. He has used those years of experience in writing this booklet.

Printed in Great Britain
by Amazon